LIBRARY

I go into my library and all history rolls before me.

ALEXANDER SMITH

LIBRARY

THE DRAMA WITHIN

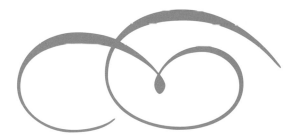

PHOTOGRAPHS BY DIANE ASSÉO GRILICHES

ESSAY BY DANIEL J. BOORSTIN

University of New Mexico Press Albuquerque

in association with the Center for the Book in the Library of Congress, Washington, D.C.

Library of Congress Cataloging-in-Publication Data
Griliches, Diane Asséo, 1931-
Library : the drama within / photographs by Diane Asséo Griliches;
essay by Daniel J. Boorstin. — 1st ed.
p.   cm.
"In association with the Center for the Book
in the Library of Congress."
ISBN 0-8263-1693-X (cloth)
1. Libraries—Pictorial works.
I. Boorstin, Daniel J. (Daniel Joseph), 1914-
II. Center for the Book. III. Title.
Z665.G864 1996
027'.0022'2—dc20   95-41804

Duotone separations, printing, and binding
by Sung In Printing Company, Korea
Printed on 150gsm Velvet Art stock
Designed by Kristina Kachele

FRONTISPIECE. Biblioteca Classense, Ravenna, Italy

CONTENTS

But what is more important in a library

than anything else

than everything else

is the fact that it exists.

ARCHIBALD MACLEISH

Preface and Acknowledgments

I am frequently asked how I happened on the idea of photographing libraries. The truth is that it came to me at three o'clock in the morning, but this does not satisfy. And it is a fact that though it seemed to creep up out of the blue, I was a quarry ready to be charmed. The path was opened by my love of books and my great fondness for libraries, one of the very few institutions on earth where any soul may walk through its doors free, and depart enriched.

I was also moved by the beauty of libraries. In contrast to many recently built ones, most libraries built in years past had artistic significance. They were symbols of optimism and civic pride. With their inspiring architecture, fine woodwork, walls lined with books, bronze lamps, sculpture, and murals, one was surrounded by greatness, a greatness matching the collection of intellectual treasures within. Though many newer libraries may have a more "democratic" look, they are often plainly utilitarian, and one learns less from them about beauty.

But that is only the setting. It is usually the people who make the scene that creates the drama. And what is in the scene that might interest a photographer? Schopenhauer said that the business of the novelist is not to chronicle great events but to make small ones interesting. This is the task of the photographer as well, and in libraries, be they old or new, the number of small events, or dramatic human moments, is infinite. The game is to pay attention, capture them, and bring them home alive.

Usually I had the luxury of plenty of time to wander about a library, soaking up the ambience before exposing my film. But occasionally I had to act quickly, with a nervous host looking over my shoulder. And sometimes I had to wait hours for a particular effect. I used only ambient light, often a tripod, and if the camera sitting on it blinked too slowly, those caught walking about might show up as "ghosts."

I went pretty far afield in my pursuit of images. When traveling in the United States, the *American Library Directory* was my constant companion, as it lists almost every library in the country. I also followed tips from the locals, both here and abroad, taking some delightful by-ways. The anecdotes accompanying the photographs are a way of sharing these experiences with the reader, and of giving a little information on particular libraries.

In my reading I had come across many stirring passages that expressed, in different ways, how unique this institution is. So I decided to become matchmaker, joining word to image, in the hope that a good union would communicate more than either could alone. Often words so evoked a particular photograph that they sprang from the page to propose marriage, without my aid. I now have a bulging file of unwed but eager candidates. Alas. Authors owe a great deal to libraries, and have written many words about them.

This book has been some six years in the making. There were ups and downs, hits and misses, and a few rough patches. But from quarry to hunter to matchmaker to midwife, it has been a most fulfilling project.

People who love books and want the public to love books must be good people. There are unsung heroes in every field, and I now sing out to those generous, lively, and unusual librarians who have been incredibly helpful, taking me in and sharing their rich world with me. Without them there might be no libraries for the people, or this book.

I also want to thank all those whom I photographed. It is through you that one can see the importance and the vitality of what goes on inside the libraries.

The photographs are arranged with their emotional impact in mind, and not in any thematic order. My intentions were not to create a documentary but a moving body of work, and what stirred me, I photographed. I have the hope that the viewer will be moved as well.

During the course of this project many gave me encouragement, critiques, suggestions, and assurance of its worth. I am first indebted to Zvi Griliches and the N + 1 Photography Group. I especially want to thank Richard Wendorf for his early appreciation of and continued faith in my work. Adonis Yatchew, with his gift of language, helped grace my text. Susan Flannery, friend and librarian supreme, let her eyes water over when my photographs moved her, and I knew I was doing something right. Dan and Pearl Bell, and Sonia and David Landes often indulged me when I needed enlightened connections or advice. I am grateful to Marge Leibenstein for sending me to Anne Edelstein, and just for being there. Lillian Bulwa, in her inimitable way had lively ideas to stir into the pot, and Jane Rabb was enthusiastic and helpful. I appreciate James Lewis for the pleasure of his company, Rodney Armstrong for not hating photographers (at least not this one), Roger Stoddard for his encouragement, and Katherine Dibble for her assistance and enthusiasm. And I am grateful to Neilita Landau in Italy, Sylvalin Edgerton in Santa Barbara, Kato Halevi, Nurit Yaari, Dalia Ofer, and Haim Regev in Jerusalem, Connie Hunt in Chicago, Toshi Jinushi in Kobe, Elena Sartore in Venice, Jacques Mairesse and Sylvia Goodenough in Paris, Ani Karasik in Tel Aviv, and Hisham Awartani in Tulkarm, Gloria Gerig in Chelsea, and Renée Copes in Los Angeles, all of whom accompanied me "on locations," and helped in other ways. The enthusiasm and support of Merle Goldman has been a constant delight to me. George Finlay and the Studley Press deserve credit for the beautifully printed prospectus of my work that made its way out into the pre-book world. Ellen Graf lent me her smiles and help, John Guillemin his time and muscle, and Pam Matz her pleasant expertise in mounting the exhibitions of this work. I treasure Nel Bundy for the memorable Virginia explorations, and for her knowledgeable company. I will remember the late John Sullivan for an amazing personal tour inside the bowels of the Library of Congress, Dr. Charles Mould for an enlightening tour of the Bodleian, and the late Dr. William

A. Moffett for showing me the life inside the Huntington. I thank Dan Griffin and Ellen Birnbaum for their suggestions, the admirable Kim Charleson at the Perkins for her patience, Marie-Therese Varlamoff at the Bibliothèque Nationale for her assistance, Jean Guillemin for her thoughtful suggestions, Carl Fleischhauer at the Library of Congress, Wilfred Beckerman in Oxford, and Elena Levin and the late Professor Harry Levin for their responsiveness and help, Professor Ivan Banic for his hospitality in Split, and András Riedlmayer and Naza Tanovic-Miller for their invaluable assistance in regard to the Sarejevo Library. There are those excellent librarians Elli Garvey, Roger Hecht, Priscilla Beck, Martha Hamilton, Daryl Marks, Ruth Dillon, Elaine McLean, Linda Murphy, Nancy Hurxthal, Kathy Fitzgerald, Catherine Sauer, William Henderson, Robert Behra, Anthony Keys, Ronnie Wise, Srs. Mary Rose Obholz and Clarina Doss, Robert Sheldon, Inez Lynn, Scot Allyn, Katherine Phillips, Charlotte S. Moman, Vivian Crysell, Beth Koostra, Lisa von Kann and Perry Viles, who came into the picture at crucial points, and contributed so much in their individual ways. Thanks to Tony Williams in Virginia, Peter Persic in Los Angeles, and Peter Casey in New York for their help. I'm sorry that Don Kunitz, one of the most language-pleasuring and idea-sharing librarians I've met, lives so far away. But I am lucky that Eve Griliches lives close by and could give me helpful comments when needed. I am very grateful to Peggy Barber of the American Library Association for past and future involvement in this project. And to my agent, the lively Anne Edelstein, who knew a good thing and acted on it, a special bouquet! At the University of New Mexico Press, it has been a pleasure to work with my solid and wise editor, Dana Asbury, who wanted to see this book happen for such a long time. Tina Kachele's designer's eye has made a most elegant presentation from my rough contributions, and Peter Moulson's know-how and energetic love of books has moved him to work on getting this one out there.

Each person mentioned here played a part in an enriching collaboration, without which this work could not have been done. And it certainly wouldn't have been as enjoyable.

Finally, a very special thanks to John Y. Cole, director of the Center for the Book in the Library of Congress, for recognizing the value of this work, for helping make possible its publication, and for his continuing involvement.

DIANE ASSÉO GRILICHES

Biblioteca Classense

The existence of a book collection in the village monastery of Classe can be traced back to 1230, but in 1515, after the Benedictine monks moved to nearby Ravenna, a genuine library came into being. The oldest part of this building dates back to that time. Thanks to the great collecting efforts of abbot-scholar Peitro Canneti, the Classense is among the most important libraries in Italy today, with a large collection of old texts and iconographic works dating back to the fifteenth century. I walked with Vice-director Dr. Dante Bolognesi (who is seen in the photograph) through some rooms with lofty ceiling frescoes, stucco reliefs, and splendid woodwork on walls lined with magnificent vellum-bound books.

The world exists
in order to become a book.
MALLARMÉ

Introduction

Libraries are exciting and inspirational places that change lives. "Libraries Change Lives," in fact, was a promotional theme developed and celebrated throughout the country in 1993 and 1994 by the American Library Association and the Center for the Book in the Library of Congress. A traveling exhibit featured testimonials by famous citizens—including Barbara Bush, Sandra Day O'Connor, Jesse Brown, Ed Bradley, and Erma Bombeck—and a hands-on display demonstrated how new technologies have found a home in most libraries.

With online services, CD-ROMs, and the Internet, not to mention videos, recordings, and works-of-art that can be borrowed, libraries obviously are much more than books. Yet, as this compelling volume of photographs by Diane Asséo Griliches makes clear, somehow there is nothing quite as poignant—or meaningful—as the magic combination of library, book, and individual reader.

The Center for the Book in the Library of Congress was created by Librarian of Congress Daniel J. Boorstin in 1977 to celebrate this synergy by stimulating public interest in books, reading, and libraries. Today the Center for the Book is still pursuing the ambitious mission Boorstin assigned it eighteen years ago—and then some. It is small (four staff members), catalytic, and flexible. It relies primarily on private contributions to support its national reading promotion campaigns, television and radio messages, traveling exhibits, symposia, publications, and projects that honor distinguished citizens and accomplishments in the world of books and libraries.

The activities of the Center for the Book reach into every region of the country through a network of 30 affiliated state centers and 121 national educational and civic organizations. These reading promotion partners of the Library of Congress enlist schools, libraries, business firms, and citizens of every age in creative projects that remind Americans of the importance of books, reading, and libraries—and of the values of a society based on the printed word.

The Center for the Book is proud to present, as an introduction to this volume, an essay that is at the heart of its existence: Daniel J. Boorstin's "A Design for an Anytime, Do-It-Yourself, Energy-Free Communication Device." The "device," of course, is the book. In the essay, published in *Harper's* in 1974, one year before he became Librarian of Congress, Boorstin presents some fundamental truths about books, libraries, and the reading experience; for example, he asks what could "be more refreshing, more invigorating, more cosmopolitanizing, than the opportunity to taste the tastes of other times and places, to break out of the prison of the marketplace?"

Twenty-six years later, in the midst of today's ever-expanding computer revolution, Boorstin's description of the unique and lasting qualities of books, their "special virtues and rewards," is still valid. In spite of almost daily predictions of its demise, the book has not been rendered anachronistic by the computer, e-mail, the Internet, the World Wide Web, or even television. Instead, as it has since Gutenberg's time, the book has continued to change, adapt, and evolve.

Books are dynamic and resilient. So are libraries. The practical and emotional appeal of each is beautifully evoked in this remarkable volume.

JOHN Y. COLE
Director
The Center for the Book
in the Library of Congress

A Design for an Anytime, Do-It-Yourself, Energy-Free Communication Device

Daniel J. Boorstin

LIBRARIAN OF CONGRESS EMERITUS

Anyone alert to the problems of communication in our country today—to the scarcity of usable television channels, to the high cost of network broadcasting, to the frustrations of cable television, to the difficulties and dangers of government supervision of broadcasting, and, of course, to the energy crisis—will have no difficulty in writing his own prescription for the ideal communication device.

What we need, first of all, is a mode of communication that uses no external energy. It should have the fewest possible moving parts, should require minimal upkeep, and yet be usable in any climate at any hour of the day or night. It should not require a continuous process of broadcasting. No wire or other physical connection should be required between broadcaster and receiver, and yet reception should be static-free. There should be an unlimited number of wavelengths or channels. And, since licensing would be unnecessary, there would be no risk of government control, favoritism, or corruption. Ideally, such a device should never become obsolete, and it should last indefinitely. If all these conditions were satisfied, there would, naturally, be no need to for it to carry commercials. And (I almost forgot) the device should of course be biodegradable!

There is no better example of the technological amnesia that afflicts the most highly developed civilizations—our tendency to forget simple ways of doing things in our desperate preoccupation with complex ways of doing them—than our need to be reminded that we already possess precisely this device. The name for it (a wonderful four-letter word) is book. Having taken for our motto (and made the basis of our economy) Rube Goldberg's aphorism, "Do it the hard way," we find it hard to keep our faith in ancient and obvious ways of doing things. For example, walking (except as a specialized sport of hikers and mountaineers) is beginning to become obsolete. We now seem to take it for granted that if God had intended man to walk, He would have given him wheels. Similarly, instead of assuming (like the generations before us) that since God gave man sight, He must have intended him to read, we make the more sophisticated (and far more American) assumption that since God gave man sight, He must have intended him to watch television.

But one of the unpredicted by-products of our sophisticated, attenuated lives is our unprecedented opportunity to rediscover the charm, the wonder, and the delight of the anciently familiar. We now have, of course, elaborated communication with un-imagined new devices—electric, electronic, phonographic, and photographic. We have complicated the machinery of sending messages in fantastic new ways in order to make it possible for everyone to receive messages effortlessly in his own home simply by turning a knob and opening his eyes. What other people has invested billions of its social capital in the machinery and organization of a new style of broadcasting in order to persuade each citizen in his living or dining room of the marginal advantages of one kind of deodorant or a foolproof new way of ridding dogs of fleas? And yet, all this may make us the first generation qualified to grasp so poignantly the wonder-ful, the uncanny, the mystic simplicity of the book.

Since the book can accomplish (and has for millennia been accomplishing) all those things I have prescribed as most desirable in a mode of communication—and which lie beyond the powers of television—is it any wonder that civilized peoples have tended to treat the written and the printed word as somehow sacred? The hieroglyph, per-haps the earliest form of writing, meant "sacred inscription." The major religions of the world have been cults of the book (or of certain books). Sacred scriptures are vehi-cles and preservers of the holy and ineffable. But while we should be newly qualified to see the providential power and simplicity of the book, other tendencies of modern American life have blurred our vision. Most striking is our passion for novelty. This passion perverts our view of history and distorts our view of all social process. It seduces us into what I call the Displacive Fallacy.

Our faith in progress leads us to assume that the bad is always, if gradually, being displaced by the good, and the good is being displaced by the better. The advertising industry—in fact our whole competitive, obsolescence-oriented economy—depends on our being persuaded that this assumption is correct so that we will buy accordingly. We are inclined to take the annual model as the prototype of industrial progress.

We readily assume that a new technology for any purpose—for transportation, communication, eradication—has the same effect on the older technology that this year's model of automobile, lawn mower, washing machine, or refrigerator, has on last year's. Another widespread misapplication of the idea of progress is, of course, the spreading institution of divorce, which seems to be based on the assumption that in marriage, too, novelty is not only for the better, but also makes the older model obsolete.

Now, the Displacive Fallacy is the belief that a new technology necessarily displaces the old. It is the belief uttered both by the unimaginative opponents of the new, and by the fanatical champions of the new. It is the belief, uttered by some pundits in the late nineteenth century, that the inevitable consequence of the telephone would be to make the U.S. mail service superfluous. (Few could predict that the service might become decadent before it had quite matured.) It is at the root of the question asked at the introduction of radio in the early years of this century—if people could send messages by wireless, why would anybody use the telephone? It is the confident prophecy, expressed by many at the diffusion of television in the 1940s, that television would be the death of radio, or that radio and television would make newspapers unnecessary. And, nowadays we hear it in the voices of the dogmatic Cassandras who insist that the rise of motion pictures, radio, and television will spell the death of the book.

We Americans (who, of all people, should be alert to the unpredictability of history) have, of all people, been the most impatient to write the obituary of any technology once it appears to have saturated the market. Of course, a few of these obituaries (e.g., of the horse as a means of transportation) turn out to be confirmed by the facts of history, but most of them have proved spectacularly premature. Not many (and perhaps not enough) Americans have expressed the cautious conservatism of a Boston friend of mine, who still refuses to install a telephone in his house: he says he is waiting until it is perfected. We might all be better social scientists and more cautious consumers if we once recognized that the moving obituaries that we read every year for last year's model are simply a characteristically American form of advertising.

The Displacive Fallacy fails to take account of an everyday phenomenon we have all witnessed. Every great innovation in technology creates a new environment for all earlier technologies, and so gives surprising new roles to earlier techniques. The telephone, which assumed many of the earlier roles of the postal service, also created new roles for the mail, and then made it possible for the mail to create additional roles for the telephone. Most recently, of course, television gave a new role to radio, which had already acquired new functions to serve the automobile. And then we have seen how the special newscasting capacities of radio and television have drawn the newspapers into novel investigative roles. Now, when television in the United States has become universal, we begin to be qualified to describe and assess some of the dangers of the Displacive Fallacy applied to books.

By now there is enough evidence to persuade even the most cautious historian that the book is not about to be displaced. The fact that writing has survived and increased in use in the five thousand years since its introduction, or that the printed book has a five-hundred-year career of increasingly widespread use, is not conclusive proof that writing or the book will be used forever. Still, there are only a few other inventions (perhaps including the wheel) which have proved so durable and so able to survive other changes in the condition of man. Publishing statistics show that more than thirty-seven thousand new works or new editions are issued each year in the United States, with the secular trend stable or slightly increasing. U.S. copyright statistics show the number of books, pamphlets, and similar items copyrighted increased between 1960 and 1970 by nearly 50 percent, from some sixty thousand to almost ninety thousand. The increase in copyrighted issues of periodicals was nearly as great.

There are some peculiarities of the book which make it more difficult to displace than other devices, especially other modes of communication. Some of these I enumerated in my prescription for an ideal communication device. Perhaps most important is a book's independence from external (artificial) sources of energy (unlike a motion picture machine, a radio, or a television set). The energy that makes a book communicate is natural energy, and is within the reader himself. Unlike some of these other devices, the book combines in itself both the broadcasting and the receiving device. While from one point of view this is a peculiar limitation of the book, it also can be one of the main obstacles to its displacement as a mode of communication. Since a radio or television set can receive any message emitted by a broadcaster, this versatility, of course, limits the market for sets. But each book, on the contrary, brings a unique message, and only that message. So long as there are new and unique messages which can be put into books, and so long as there are people who do not possess the books containing all the old messages, the market for books has not been saturated. And since the market for books can probably never be saturated, the device itself cannot be displaced.

A further feature of the book is that old and foreign models—the books of other times and places—do not necessarily become obsolete or unmarketable. Old books are unlike old movies in that their enjoyment need not be confined to hours after midnight. And time and changing events automatically give an old book a new charm. There is no technological obstacle (comparable to the problem of playing 78 rpm records on 33 rpm machines) to the diffusion and reception of the message.

Moreover, some books, like some ski slopes, can be negotiated by only a few. This limitation on the audience of books is especially significant. For in our democratic society nearly everything else is supposed to be for everybody, and is evaluated (and usually rewarded) in proportion to its capacity to reach everybody. Books remain perhaps the last refuge for communication of the subtle, the difficult, the profound—in brief, for what cannot, should not, and need not be communicated to everyone. The more the rest of the communication in our society becomes communication to everybody—the more people are dominated by TV, self-explanatory images, the vernacular word—the more distinctive and essential is this role of the book.

Even so, numerous perils threaten to corrupt the book, and instead of allowing it to be a tonic to our society, tend to infect it with the weaknesses of the society as a whole. They are the countless ways of assimilating the book to the other, more characteristic, forms of communication of our age. We see the premium on novelty, and need not go far to observe those whom John Webster, back in the seventeenth century, called the "ignorant asses visiting stationer's shops . . . not to inquire for good books, but new books." We see the symptoms of excess. Publishers must fill their lists to reduce the unit overhead. It costs no more for a salesman to tout fifty new titles than to tout five. There is the appeal of the ersatz, the nonbooks, the compilations, pseudo-biographies, parasitic books (which live off living books), and sapro-phytic books (which live off dead authors and dead books). But these, by their very effort to masquerade as books, still somehow testify to the prestige of the book. And then there is the myopia, the preoccupation with the here and now, the strenuous effort to produce books that have all the triviality and transience of a newspaper, or of the latest televised gossip. All this is, of course, much too obvious to need under-lining.

Perhaps less obvious are the special virtues and rewards of books which now appear in the peculiar circumstance of our age. We suddenly discover anew all the things a book is not. Books are not motion pictures or radio broadcasts or television programs. I can think of at least four newly revealed virtues of the book, which make it unique both for the author and the audience.

FOR THE AUTHOR:

(1) *The book is a do-it-yourself thing.* By contrast to the more industrially and technologically elaborated media, the book is the freest and most open of avenues. Movies, radio programs, and television programs require expensive and complicated equipment. To reach a large audience an author's manuscript must, of course, be pub-lished, and the size of the audience depends to some extent on the power and resources and energy of the publisher. Nevertheless, anybody with meager and inexpensive equipment (pencil and paper will do!) can make the product for publication. By con-trast with every other known substance for communication, the manuscript for a book is a do-it-yourself thing. Motion pictures, radio, and television are the easiest media for totalitarian governments to control, but books are among the hardest. A book can be written in privacy, or in secrecy. Some great and powerful books have been writ-

ten in prison. The equipment is easy to secure, hard to trace. It is no accident that the voices of protest from the dictatorships of our time are heard not in motion pictures or on radio or television, but in secretly written manuscripts which become books. Moreover, the manuscript of a book is portable and durable. If it is not published today, it can be published next year; if *Dr. Zhivago* cannot be published in the U.S.S.R., it can be published in Finland, France, or the United States. In free countries, too, the bookish (printed) product of an age offers a far wider spectrum of thought, belief, disbelief, passion, and poetry than can be found in its movies, over its radios, or on its television screens. The more costly, the more centralized, the more elaborate the other media become, the more distinctive and the more precious is this do-it-yourself medium.

(2) *The book is a refuge of the noncollaborative.* "The book is mine." So wrote novelist Calder Willingham, who had spent the first ten years of his career writing novels and stories, and much of the next fifteen years writing movie scripts. He had not been underpaid for his work as a screenwriter (for some periods in 1970 he was paid $26,250 per week), at least by contrast with his time spent writing his novels (he figures this at about $260 per week). But, after a considerable, and not unsuccessful, career as a screenwriter, Willingham valued his freedom more than ever—his freedom as an author. Here is his eloquent conclusion:

> Yes, mind-boggling, breath-taking and dazzling, the gold in them thar "Cuckoo-land" hills. The catch is that the work is not yours. Producers, director, stars and even cigar-smoking, starlet-grabbing studio executives feel perfectly competent to "fix" a screenplay. They pay you a small fortune to write it and then they can't wait to get their cotton-pickin' hands on it and "fix" it. A mad logic, there. And even when they do not "fix" it . . . the interpretation of the director can alter out of all recognition your original intent.

Novels are for writers. Writing them is a hellish labor, true, but, a printer has never yet said to my publisher: "I am not going to print that chapter, because I simply don't feel it." I have heard that sinister comment more than a little in the golden realm of film. As Jocko de Paris in "End as a Man" observed to Sowbelly Simmons: "You're a hairy little bastard, but you're all mine." How true. No matter how hateful the reviews and no matter how sad the sales, the book is mine.

In our collaborative age, then, in our age of committees and conventions and foundation grants (awarded by competent and cautious committees), in our age of publicized and democratized production of everything, the book (despite the sometimes sinister efforts of publishers and editors) remains an island of individualism, the utopia of the noncollaborator.

FOR THE READER:

(3) *The book is an anytime thing.* While the good television program is a sometime thing, good books are always ready for use at our convenience. It is conceivable that cable television and cassette movies may neutralize the limitations of the projector and the broadcast screen, but that time is still not in sight. And it will take centuries to provide a range of choice and a stock of classics to rival the vast accumulation of books. Moreover, because the book has been the classic form for the narrative and philosophic statements of past ages, all that the motion picture or television screen can ever offer us is a translation. Messages from all past times and places, while always imperfect, ambiguous, and iridescent, still come to us more directly in the book than in any other form. The book is an anytime thing in two senses. It brings us messages (in the actual medium of that age) from anytime past. And its message is receivable at any time in the present. No number of channels can offer us this bookish range of choice or this convenience.

(4) *The book is a residual thing, the refuge of the un-market-researched product.* Television reinforces our current interests; books remind us of what interested all times and places. The fantastic elaborations of market research simply increase this relative advantage of our stock of books. Nowadays nearly everything we see and use and buy, the ads we read, the slogans we hear, the commercials we are shown, the products we are offered, have been pretested to be sure that we are offered only what we want, or think we want. The more up-to-date, the more fluid and more rapidly advancing our system of production becomes, the less opportunity we are offered for the pleasures of the time tested, the obsolete, and the residual. If you want to buy the kind of toothbrush you bought and liked two years ago, or the shirt with the peculiar mix of Dacron or nylon that you bought and liked last year, the chances are that you won't find it. At least not if it was produced by an up-to-the-minute manufacturer, and marketed by an enterprising retailer.

In our astonishing civilization, where the good is always being supplanted by the new, and the new by the newer, where the sign of prosperity is the ability to discard the still-usable, there remains one warehouse where there are readily available the models of *any* earlier period or *any* place (tariff or no tariff, common market or not). That is the world of books. Our bookstores, especially in their vast stocks of paperbacks, offer reprints of books that are not this year's, or even this century's model. What publishers once called the Paperback Revolution should more properly be called the Paperback Resurrection. The paperback has brought back from the dead many books to inform, to delight, to astonish, and to shock. And, of course, the decline of the second-hand bookstore gives the library a more important role than ever before. Libraries offer the largest stock of old-fashioned models of anything available anywhere in our novelty-prone country. What can be more refreshing, more invigorating, more cosmopolitanizing, than the opportunity to taste the tastes of other times and places, to break out of the prison of our marketplace?

Instant obsolescence is the charm, the surprise, and the outrage of the American standard of living. Yet there is nothing more provincial or more transient than the up-to-the-minute vision. Never did a people more need the book. For the book is our de-provincializing machine.

The Photographs

Widener Library

HARVARD UNIVERSITY, CAMBRIDGE, MASSACHUSETTS

A poster of Berenice Abbott's photograph of James Joyce is inside an office door, illuminated by daylight from the office windows. Professor Harry Levin, the late James Joyce scholar, found the quotation for me. The Widener houses the Harvard College Library, which had its beginnings in 1638 when thirty-one-year-old John Harvard, as he lay dying of consumption, bequeathed some 400 books along with his name to the new college. It is the largest university library in the world, and students and scholars have the privilege and pleasure of free access to the open stacks.

.... *the studious silence of the library* ...
Tranquil brightness.
JAMES JOYCE

William Rainey Harper Memorial Library

NORTH READING ROOM, UNIVERSITY OF CHICAGO,
CHICAGO, ILLINOIS

The beautiful large Gothic campus was built in the 1890s on a flat and treeless plain, creating its own landscape there. The English collegiate architecture provided reassurance to any skeptical trustees, and a reminder that those working within its walls were subordinate to the goals of the university as a whole. And there is the wonderful idiosyncrasy of its medieval art forms: gargoyles hover on the edges as shadows from the Gothic arches play on the modern lounges. William Rainey Harper was the university's first president. The North Reading Room, called the "Romper Room" by the students, is under threat of being taken over by the Graduate School of Business for their own use. Students are clamoring to keep it just as it is, fighting what is said to be a losing battle.

They passed into the medieval hush of the Reading Room. The stained glass was casting greens and blues with the light of a perpetual twelfth century afternoon, and the sense of another time washed over them.

CHARLES A. GOODRUM

John Fitzgerald Kennedy Library

DORCHESTER, MASSACHUSETTS

I. M. Pei's geometric structure on the exterior of his building is seen from within the research library. The library's primary documents, available for research here, include the recently released tape recordings of President Kennedy and his advisors dealing with the Cuban Missile Crisis, and Theodore White's notes from the "Camelot" interview with Jacqueline Kennedy.

The age of Lincoln and Jefferson memorials is over. It will be presidential libraries from now on. —ADA LOUISE HUXTABLE

23

Kobe University Library

KOBE, JAPAN

There were three Japanese students giggling in front of this photograph when it was on exhibit in Boston. They must have had the same problem staying awake while studying. The library survived the recent devastating earthquake in Kobe, although thirty-nine students lost their lives.

An afternoon nap, while not exactly
condoned, is at least tolerated in the
spirit of humanitarian laissez-faire.

BRUCE A. SHUMAN

Redwood Library and Athenaeum
NEWPORT, RHODE ISLAND

This is the oldest circulating library in the country that still operates in its original location. It was built in 1748 by Peter Harrison, the architect of Newport's Touro Synagogue, the oldest surviving synagogue in America. Readers may sit in a cozy corner, surrounded by an important collection of portrait paintings, busts, eighteenth-century furniture, and a book collection with major strengths in the arts and humanities, most of which circulates. Subscribers pay a small annual fee for the privilege of enjoying these amenities.

A bookcase is as good as a view, as the sight of a city or a river. —ANATOLE BROYARD

Read meanwhile . . .
Hunt among the shelves,
as dogs do grasses . . .
RANDALL JARRELL

Newton Free Library

NEWTON, MASSACHUSETTS

When I got my library card, that's when my life began.
RITA MAE BROWN

Boston Symphony Orchestra Library

BOSTON, MASSACHUSETTS

Pictured here are Vic Firth, the BSO tympanist, and Marty Burlingame, the orchestra librarian, two very funny fellows who made me laugh while trying to hold the camera steady. Mr. Burlingame described the ensemble library as a repository of human thought and genius. He says that one can gain insight into the personality of a particular orchestra by studying its instrumental parts, for each set has a myriad of pencil markings indicating bowings, dynamics, and other signs of expression and interpretation. These markings reveal the unique sonorous profile of the orchestra as well as the personality of the conductor. The library, which has been here for close to one hundred years, is accessible to players at all times. They come into this beautiful room to study parts or just to enjoy its ambience, as did Arthur Fiedler, who had his own desk in the library and spent a good deal of time here.

In a library we are surrounded by many hundreds of dear friends imprisoned by an enchanter in paper and leathern boxes.

RALPH WALDO EMERSON

Massachusetts Correctional Institution Law Library
NORFOLK, MASSACHUSETTS

The library is in the medium security prison where Malcolm X was held. He was transferred to Norfolk on the request of his sister, since the library and the educational-rehabilitation program are its outstanding features. Malcolm X started by slowly reading a dictionary from beginning to end, copying out each entry. He went from there to reading and understanding books for the first time. "My alma mater was books and a good library. I don't think anybody ever got more out of going to prison than I did."

Ten guards and the warden couldn't have torn me out of those books. Months passed without even thinking about being imprisoned. . . . I had never been so truly free in my life.

MALCOLM X

Noxubee County Library

MACON, MISSISSIPPI

It was built (in Romanesque style) as a jail in 1907. When the old jail was closed a few years ago, the present head librarian, Beth Koostra, led a campaign with the citizens of Macon to raise funds to convert it into a library. Their efforts were heroic, given the poverty of this area. They were also determined to preserve its unique "decor," and, along with the barred cells, a rope hook and trap door for the gallows were left on the third floor.

Why is there not a Majesty's Library in every county town? There is a Majesty's gaol in every one. —THOMAS CARLYLE

New York Public Library

NEW YORK CITY

I stood on the sidewalk watching the citizens of America walking by, walking
in, walking out, or just hanging around on the steps, people-watching like me.
Carriere and Hastings, the library's architects, were once draftsmen for McKim,
Mead and White, who built the Boston Public and Pierpont Morgan Libraries.
The New York Public Library celebrated its 100th birthday in 1995.

Hey, young man, hurrying by, a Walkman plugged into your skull: pause a moment,
mount those steps and enter. The world awaits you. —PETE HAMILL

New York Public Library, Reading Room 315

NEW YORK CITY

Despite the comings and goings of the patrons, the atmosphere of this monumental Reading Room is one of quiet intensity. This commodious space has nurtured generations of writers and scholars, and given comfort and knowledge to many an ordinary citizen. As I observed the readers here, ferreting out and feeding off the printed page, the noise and the craziness of Fifth Avenue and 42nd Street, just outside, seemed a world away.

I liked reading and working out my ideas in the midst of that endless crowd walking in and out of 315 looking for Something.
ALFRED KAZIN

The Huntington Library

It began life as a "gentleman's library," part of the estate of the millionaire Henry E. Huntington. His exemplary collections of rare books and manuscripts make it a leading research library. I visited here in 1991, shortly after Director William A. Moffett made a stunning announcement: in accordance with the research library's mission, their complete set of 3,000 photographic negatives of the Dead Sea Scrolls would be made available to all qualified researchers. He thus broke the cartel of a small team of international editors who have had tight control of the actual scrolls. The scholar here uses the cradles and book-weights that are common in a rare book reading room to help preserve the books.

Time is conferred on those who seek to unravel the mysteries of these books and documents before their historical evidence disappears.
RICHARD WENDORF

The Library of Congress,
Rare Book Conservation Section
WASHINGTON, D.C.

This is a huge operation where the library's damaged manuscripts and books are resuscitated. Tom Albro, the head of the section, likens the conservators to "ancient craftsmen." This certainly did seem a sort of monks' work, involving the reverence, skill, dedication, and patience rare and admirable in our age. The manuscript here appears to be a legal text in a combination of Catalan and Latin.

By all rights, it should be dust. But through the rescue work . . . the book has been preserved. —LINTON WEEKS

National and University Library of Israel

JERUSALEM, ISRAEL

I had little light and used a slow shutter, not expecting this Hasidic scholar to move so soon. The camera caught him mid-flight with a tray from the card catalogue.

*There was something . . . that made me restless with
the need to grab up every book, press into every
single mind right there on the open shelves.*
ALFRED KAZIN

The Queens Borough Public Library

JAMAICA, NEW YORK

This library has the highest circulation of books in the country. It is in a multiethnic, immigrant neighborhood, and the streets are a wild mass of shop signs in many languages. On that Saturday the place was bustling with the regulars, and with new immigrants who can learn to read English, get a driver's license, find a job, start a business, take the college entrance exams, use a computer, and check out books and videos in several languages—all under one roof and free of cost.

They go in not because they need any certain volume but because they feel that there may be some book that needs them.
CHRISTOPHER MORLEY

Monroeville County Public Library

MONROEVILLE, ALABAMA

These kids were volunteers here. One teen took me to the nearby old courthouse that figures in Harper Lee's *To Kill a Mockingbird,* the 1960 book (later a play) about racial bigotry in this town. A group of talented black and white actors from the community were rehearsing the play for its yearly performance, right there in the old Monroe County Courtroom. The performance was so convincing, I thought I'd walked into an actual trial. In talking with the actors afterward, I got the impression that things have improved here since the time the book was written.

Is this the place where I ask questions I can't get the answers to? —WILLIAM COLE

Perkins School for the Blind Library

WATERTOWN, MASSACHUSETTS

The book markers give the braille library a unique appearance. The Perkins also has a tremendous selection of unabridged books on tape from the Library of Congress, which it mails to the blind, lending out a four-track tape recorder as well, all free of charge.

As long as I can read, nothing human is beyond my understanding, nothing is totally foreign to my nature . . . there are no limits to my being . . . I'm never alone.

LINDA WELTNER

Beverly Hills Public Library

BEVERLY HILLS, CALIFORNIA

The corridor to the Children's Room is called the "Time Tunnel." Its arches diminish in size and increase in color intensity to suggest a "down-the-rabbit-hole" feeling. This is the work of architect Charles Moore. In 1990 he remodeled and expanded the original library building. The kids seemed to love making the run down "the Tunnel."

I was there on a more exciting mission:
the discovery of the world.
PETE HAMILL

Boston Public Library, Bates Reading Room

BOSTON, MASSACHUSETTS

After reading at one of the tables for a while, you begin to realize that there are all these other people around you, soaking up books just like you, something like being in a sauna together. Bates Reading Room was named for John Bates, whose story is endearing and significant. As a youth, having no money to buy books nor heat for his room, he was indebted to a Boston bookseller who gave him a warm corner in which to read the store's merchandise free. The self-educated boy became a wealthy man in England, with a partnership in the (recently failed) Baring Brothers Bank. Bates knew the value of free access to books and became the new library's first great and essential benefactor, on the condition that it be "Free to All." These words are carved over the main portal of the library. In 1852 it was the first public library in a large city to be supported by citizens' taxes. Every year two million of these citizens come through its doors, even more than the Red Sox manage to draw.

In the reading room . . . they are inside the books.
They move sometimes within the pages,
like sleepers turning over between two dreams.

RAINER MARIA RILKE

Boston Public Library

BOSTON, MASSACHUSETTS

This solid, well-used wooden veteran has a personal attraction and a kind of lasting beauty that a computer can never have. I wanted to make its portrait before it disappears.

For me the card catalogue has been a companion
all my working life. To leave it is like leaving the
house one was brought up in.

BARBARA TUCHMAN

The Library of Congress, Main Reading Room

WASHINGTON, D.C..

This view from Shakespeare's foot looks down from under a 160-foot-high dome. The Library of Congress, housed in three buildings near the U.S. Capitol building, is the largest in the world. The magnitude of its holdings and activities is mind-boggling. Each day, 31,000 new items come into its mailroom. Its vast collection includes historical artifacts and documents, photographs, maps, rare books, personal papers, recordings, and other creative products of humanity. Its twenty-one reading rooms are open to the public. With its 110 million items, which includes approximately 20 million books, the Library of Congress is the most comprehensive collection of knowledge in the world. It also administers the operation of the U.S. copyright law, which encourages artistic and literary endeavors, like the making of this book.

Even the brashest tourist speaks in a whisper. What goes on here, he perceives instinctively, matches the majesty of the surroundings.
PAUL ANGLE

The Folger Shakespeare Library

WASHINGTON, D.C.

Shakespeare presides over the readers, pleased that his work continues to fascinate. Amazingly, the world's largest collection of Shakespeareana resides right here. Henry Clay Folger traveled the path from impecunious student to chairman of the board of Standard Oil. Both he and his wife, Emily Jordan Folger, had a passion for Shakespeare and spent a lifetime collecting these treasures. When they decided to give them to the American public, Congress voted to build the Folger Library as a major research center. The architect, Paul Philippe Cret, designed an interior evocative of the Elizabethan era.

Come, take choice of all my library, and so beguile thy sorrow. —WILLIAM SHAKESPEARE

Houghton Library, Hyde Oval Exhibition Room, Harvard University

CAMBRIDGE, MASSACHUSETTS

Its eighteenth-century English literature collection, delicately illuminated, the cast-in-London plaster ceiling, and Italian marble floor are all a part of the beautiful room created by Mary Hyde (now the Vicountess Eccles) in memory of her first husband, Donald Hyde. Samuel Johnson's portraits preside over this room, and the one on the far wall is by Sir Joshua Reynolds. Mary Hyde Eccles has the largest collection of Johnsoniana in the world, and it includes many other images of Dr. Johnson.

*My dream was to live in this heavenly building and know all its secrets . . . to be allowed to go behind
the curving book-clad walls into the stacks and have keys to unlock the cabinets of bookish rarities.*
GERMAINE GREER

The Boston Athenaeum

BOSTON, MASSACHUSETTS

Built in 1849, this was Boston's principal library until the opening of the Boston Public Library. It now has some 5,000 members and a magnificent collection that distinguishes it as a research library. "Athenaion" was a temple dedicated to the goddess Athena, where poets came to read their works aloud. This, however, is a very quiet reading room. Rodney Armstrong, the Athenaeum's director and librarian, was generous in allowing me to make photographs here, as, he says, the library's members feel it to be an extension of their own homes and lives.

.... *the papered memorial of mankind.* —ARTHUR SCHOPENHAUER

Pembroke Public Library

I found this library only because I was chatting with a customer at a local an-
tiques store who happened to be the president of the County Historical Society.
He sent me to this little library that used to be the town's post office. It is certainly the tiniest library I've ever seen, and with five people inside, I had to
stay outside and photograph.

*The library is a place where most of the things
I came to value as an adult had their beginnings.*
PETE HAMILL

Emma Yates Memorial Library

POCAHONTAS, VIRGINIA

When Emma Yates died, the family turned over her hat store to the people of this small coal-mining town to convert to a library of donated books, run by two volunteer librarians. While lunching at the local cafe with them, they suggested I get the key from the postmistress and visit the old Opera House. I, a total stranger, was given the key, but on the way was hailed into the town store where three men sat around a pot-bellied stove. One insisted on giving me a personal tour of the Opera House, now used as a community activities center.

A library is books and somewhere to put them and some people to want them there . . . —SHEILA BOURBEAU

Tulkarm Public Municipal Library

TULKARM, PALESTINE

In the library I discovered that you could learn by following your nose. And I learned that a book was as close to a living thing as you could get without being one.

BILL HARLEY

If a boy wants to learn the secret of
life, you have to accommodate him.
ISAAC BASHEVIS SINGER

Tulkarm Arab
Orphanage Library
TULKARM, PALESTINE

71 ✎

Shrewsbury Bookmobile

SHREWSBURY, MASSACHUSETTS

As the library bus rounded the corner and assumed its usual place, children and adults poured out into the street. It was as attractive as an ice cream wagon.

When I . . . discovered libraries, it was like having Christmas every day! —JEAN FRITZ

Boston Public Library, Newspaper Room

BOSTON, MASSACHUSETTS

Among patrons needing current or back issues of newspapers are those (usually men) who make a ritual of coming in to read the daily papers. This same gentleman was here two years later when I came by.

. . . the riffle of pages being turned in the Periodicals Room where the old men hung out,
reading newspapers which had been threaded into long sticks.

STEPHEN KING

Harry Elkins Widener Memorial Room,
Widener Library

HARVARD UNIVERSITY, CAMBRIDGE, MASSACHUSETTS

This is the Gutenberg Bible purchased for Harry Elkins Widener by his father while the son was abroad. He was never to return, going down with the *Titanic* in 1912. The Widener Library was erected with the support of Eleanor Elkins Widener in memory of her son, who was an ardent bibliophile, and this Memorial Room contains his own priceless library, which is accessible for research. From his place high on the far wall, Harry Elkins Widener keeps an eye on the Gutenberg Bible, once stolen from this room but quickly recovered when the thief, with the books in his knapsack, fell from a rope as he tried to escape.

Gutenberg has marked the transition
of man-slave to the free-man.
VICTOR HUGO

Pierpont Morgan Library

NEW YORK CITY

Dwight Peters was on a class field trip from Brooklyn to the Morgan Library. I doubt he'd ever seen a book like this medieval illuminated manuscript. The library, an Italianate palazzo, designed by Charles Follen McKim, was built in 1906 by the financier and voracious collector of literature and art, J. Pierpont Morgan. In 1924 the library was made public by Morgan's son, who felt that its holdings were too important to keep private. As one guest said, "I love the Morgan . . . especially for being open to me." The collections contain masterpieces documenting man's creative achievements.

This Library has to be one of the best places to be walled up alive.

JOHN RUSSELL

Marcus Cohen Yeshiva Library

JERUSALEM, ISRAEL

Located in the Mosad Harav Kook, the library was built by the three sons of Marcus Cohen. Rav Kook was the first chief rabbi of Israel, and the Mosad is a research institute working on and publishing the manuscripts left by Rav Kook. The institute also studies many areas of Judaism.

*I'd spent hours browsing those books, groaning
like the Hasidic Fathers, rocking my bent body
back and forth till I finally made my choice.*
MICHAEL WATERS

81

Biblioteka Ivan Paštrić

SPLIT, CROATIA

A journalist told me about this seminary library as we were having coffee in the town square in Split. So we went knocking on the door. The seminarians were warm and gracious and showed us two small windowless rooms holding these musty volumes. The Communists closed the seminary but allowed the men to keep the library in these two rooms.

We had that peculiar thrill which comes from
going into a room redolent with the faint
mustiness of old calf and feeling that almost
any volume may turn out a treasure.

HAROLD J. LASKI

83

Houghton Library, Harvard University

CAMBRIDGE, MASSACHUSETTS

Here, caught at his own acquisitorial game, is the man known as the "dean of American bookmen." It is these bookmen who have the talent, knowledge, experience (and obsession?) to sense what there is about a book that makes it important enough to acquire. At a university library, the test of a librarian's acquisitions is the use scholars make of the collections. Rare Book Curator Roger Stoddard is keeping up the tradition of the Houghton Library's first director, William A. Jackson, who was called the "Grand Acquisitor."

People can lose their lives in Libraries. They ought to be warned. — SAUL BELLOW

Hungarian Library

This library is squeezed into three tiny, cluttered rooms off a small street in downtown Jerusalem. The librarian said it's difficult for Hungarian immigrants to learn Hebrew, and the old people often take out books in Hungarian that they had read in their childhood. "Perhaps they are looking for their youth," she said.

This was merchandise to be handled. If the pages were worn and dog-eared, if the card tucked into
its paper pocket inside the cover was stamped with lots of dates, I knew I had a winner! — BEL KAUFMAN

Boston Public Library, Bates Reading Room

BOSTON, MASSACHUSETTS

David Osborn was sitting there before the computer screen, another beautiful head among the marble busts of New England worthies. I asked permission to take his photograph and to send his parents a release form, since David was only seventeen. He said sure, but would I please not tell them what time he was in the library as he was supposed to be in school. (His mother now knows he was in the library, and it's OK.)

He grew dutifully, conspicuously studious, spend-
ing long afternoons in the town library, watched
over by a white plaster bust of Ben Franklin.

DAVID MCCULLOUGH

Chelsea Carnegie Public Library

CHELSEA, MASSACHUSETTS

The feeling one gets here is of service—to the children, the multiethnic patrons, and the senior citizens. This is a real community library, with useful information posted everywhere. The walls abound with portraits of its most illustrious and generous citizens. An earlier library burned down during the great Chelsea fire of 1908, but in 1910 Andrew Carnegie was persuaded to give to Chelsea the fine piece of architecture that is the library today. A weaver's son in Scotland before he made his millions, Carnegie gave money to build 3,000 library buildings during a twenty-year period, on condition that the communities take responsibility for them after that. The neighborhood library is often an important source of information for new immigrants. Carnegie was often quoted: "Libraries provide a ladder of success that does not pauperize." The portrait on the left is of the first librarian, Medora Simpson, who served for fifty years, and the one on the right is of Andrew Carnegie himself.

There was a man named Andrew
Carnegie who gave lots of money for
libraries 'cause he had been dumb once
himself and he wanted everyone to have
an equal chance like he didn't have.

NIKKI GIOVANNI

91

The London Library

This is the largest independent lending library in the world, a "private" library of five or six thousand readers. Members (anyone may join for a reasonable fee) have access to the stacks, and may borrow almost any book it owns, including old and rare ones. The Royal Family borrows by mail, and a listing of the library's members, past and present, reads like a Who's Who of the English literary world. It was founded in 1841 by Thomas Carlyle, who was fed up with existing library facilities in London. Dickens was one of its founding members, Tennyson an early president, and T. S. Eliot its president in the 1960s. The point has always been to lend out the books, and while I was there some members were borrowing them by the stackful. Its reading room, with deep leather armchairs, has the quiet and friendly atmosphere of a London club. The place inspires extraordinary affection for its atmosphere of kindness and generosity. One patron said, "If I ever get to heaven and find that it contains no celestial duplication of the London Library, I shall request an interview with God."

It has been said that England has produced three institutions at once admirable and unique. I forget what the third is; but the other two are the Monarchy and the London Library. —LORD DAVID CECIL

Calouste Gulbenkian Library
of the Armenian Patriarchate

This library is in the Armenian quarter of the Old City of Jerusalem. It was established in 1929 by Calouste Gulbenkian, a famous Armenian philanthropist, and since then it has received thousands of books from Armenia, Lebanon, Egypt, and the Armenian diaspora in the USA. One-third of the library's materials are in Armenian. The library is open for research, but it has also served as the cultural and educational center for the Armenians in Israel.

A monastery without a bookchest is like a castle without an armory. —MONK IN NORMANDY, C. 1170

St. Johnsbury Athenaeum

ST. JOHNSBURY, VERMONT

An intimate and beautiful old library with a hauntingly well-preserved Victorian art gallery, it was created in 1871 as an independent corporation and a public library. The day I visited, a group of middle-school kids came in after school to hang out, do homework, and compare Walkmans. The friendly staff made the kids feel welcome.

When I enter a Library . . .
I still have a reassuring sense
that it is going to tell me
all I need to know.

SUSAN ALLEN TOTH

Biblioteca Marucelliana

FLORENCE, ITALY

One look into this reading room and I knew it wanted to be photographed. Its high walls are lined with vellum-bound books, and on terra firma a hushed mass of students pored over their books under the green lamps. Before I was allowed to photograph I had to answer questions for an hour and a half, and sign a lengthy affidavit. This was in compliance with the new "Law 4," passed by the short-lived Berlusconi government to regulate revenues in the art world, hoping it would help shrink the Italian national debt. The 1702 will of Fr. Marucelli established this library. Since it opened in 1752 it has been supported and amplified with gifts and acquisitions of incunabulae, prints, letters, manuscripts, and books of a general character.

The student has his Rome, his Florence, his whole glowing Italy, within the four walls of his library.
He has in his books the ruins of an antique world, and the glories of a modern one.
HENRY WADSWORTH LONGFELLOW

Bibliothèque Sainte-Geneviève

PARIS, FRANCE

There is a poetic quality to this space in the early morning before it opens to the rush of university students (whom I was not allowed to photograph). In the Middle Ages, the library was housed in the Abbey of Sainte-Geneviève. The present edifice was built by Henri Labrouste (architect of the Bibliothèque Nationale), and is a reflection of the new industrial age, with its iron frame and wrought-iron decorations. It was chosen by architect Charles Follen McKim as the model for his Boston Public Library.

When I step into this library, I cannot understand why I ever step out of it. —MARIE DE SÉVIGNÉ

Boston Public Library, Courtyard

BOSTON, MASSACHUSETTS

As a warm, safe, clean, and free alternative to the streets, the library is often used as a refuge by some of the homeless, although this is not without its problems. For a few who take advantage of them, the library's resources have even been a ticket off those streets. This beautiful Italian Renaissance courtyard is open to all throughout the year. Charles Follen McKim, the library's architect, also built the Pierpont Morgan Library and the magnificent Penn Station in New York City that was shamefully demolished and replaced with today's miserable structures. The profound effect of its demise provoked the founding of the Landmarks Preservation Commission, giving it legal authority to save such architectural materpieces.

When the jailhouse ambience of the shelter became too much, I would retreat to the outdoor atrium at the Boston Public Library . . . to lose my loneliness in conversation with a stranger. —MICHAEL BRENNAN

Cleveland Depot Literacy Library

CLEVELAND, MISSISSIPPI

Built in 1884, the railroad ran from New Orleans up to Memphis, and new towns like Cleveland, Mississippi, were created along the route. President Grover Cleveland, after whom the town was named, William Jennings Bryan, and President Theodore Roosevelt made whistle stops here. The train stopped running in the 1960s. The abandoned depot was recently converted to a special Library for Adult Literacy and has three hundred students. Huey Wright, one of them, is just leaving class. Ronnie Wise, director of the County Library System, took me here, where I spent a few hours observing the work of teaching adults to read, many with the aid of computers. The next step is a better job, and perhaps checking out books from the library.

To use it should be as natural . . . as to use the trolley when one needs transportation. —JOHN COTTON DANA

University of California at Berkeley Library, Morrison
Reading Room

BERKELEY, CALIFORNIA

The Library is the Heart of the University.
CHARLES W. ELIOT

Thomas Crane Public Library

QUINCY, MASSACHUSETTS

Libraries . . those temples of learning,
those granite-and-marble monuments . . .
SUSAN ALLEN TOTH

National and University Library of Israel,
Manuscript Room

JERUSALEM, ISRAEL

It is communication across the centuries: the ancient texts, copied onto film, are accessible by the latest technology. Unlike national and university libraries generally, this one is open to the public for reference and borrowing.

Scholar examining an 11th Century manuscript
of a Hebrew translation
of an Arabic commentary
on the logic of Aristotle.

Los Angeles Central Library

LOS ANGELES, CALIFORNIA

After a terribly destructive fire in the library in 1986, there was some call to have the 1926 pyramid-topped masterwork of Bertram Goodhue razed and replaced. (When it was built, it was so magnificent that its first librarian worried it might be too distracting to readers.) Fortunately it was saved and renovated and an addition built in 1993. In the heart of the business district, it is only four stories high, and while it is surrounded by tall, sleek office towers, the library is an oasis, abounding in murals, gardens, pools, and symbols of enlightenment. This children's department has the lush Albert Herter California history murals, so that children can be inspired by both art and literature.

To my thinking, a great librarian must have a clear
head, a strong hand, and above all, a great heart . . .
and I am inclined to think that most of the men who
will achieve this greatness will be women.

MELVIL DEWEY

Bodleian Library

OXFORD, ENGLAND

When I was here to photograph this oldest part of the Bodleian, Duke Humfrey's Library, it was suffering from electrical problems, as well as from an invasion of the death-watch beetle, and was under intensive repair. The stacks were covered with plastic and were hardly photogenic, and so the photograph is taken from inside, looking out. Duke Humfrey, brother of Henry V, gave Oxford University a great collection of manuscripts. The library was built in 1488 to house the collection. The Bodleian was named after Sir Thomas Bodley, about whom King James I said, "He should be called Sir Thomas Godley!" He was an academic who, a hundred years after Duke Humfrey's library was built, dedicated a good part of his life to restoring and expanding it.

Were I not a King, I would be an University
man; and if it were so that I must be made
prisoner, I would have no other prison than
this library, and be chained together
with all these goodly authors.

JAMES I OF ENGLAND

National and University Library of Bosnia and Herzogovina in Sarajevo (now destroyed)

In August 1992, the Serbs bombed the library for three consecutive days with incendiary grenades. Only the walls now remain. Almost the entire written record of Bosnia's multicultural heritage went up in flames—one and a half million volumes, including 155,000 manuscripts and rare books. I made my photograph in 1991, not having a clue that very soon the library would be destroyed. Enes Kujundžić, the library's current director, said that this was an extremely reading-oriented population and that the Bosnian Serb forces "knew that if they wanted to destroy ('cleanse') this multiethnic society, they would have to destroy the library."

The remains of the library.
Photograph by Esad Bakira Tanović,
February 1993.

*I warned myself that it would take only a few
wars . . . or a single period of brutality or
savagery . . . to destroy forever the ideas
passed down with the help of these
frail objects in fiber and ink.*
MARGUERITE YOURCENAR

Margaret Walker Alexander Library

The library is in a shopping center, so that patrons can drop in here to "shop" for books as well. The librarian took me to meet Margaret Walker Alexander at her home near this library that is named in her honor. She is the author of several books, including *Jubilee,* a novel built around her great-grandmother's life as a slave in Georgia.

If you're rich you can buy books. If you're poor, you need a library. —JOHN KENNETH GALBRAITH

Uphams Corner Branch Library of the Boston Public Library

DORCHESTER, MASSACHUSETTS

Uphams Corner is a very tough neighborhood, but instead of being in the streets, these kids were in the library, watched over by the librarians, doing their homework, and enjoying the books until their parents came to fetch them. George May, the library's custodian, remembers when this municipal building had showers (towels and soap one cent apiece) serving residents of cold-water flats. There was also a gym and a pool. The marble-lined pool was converted to a marble-lined children's library in 1926, which is still active on the lower floor of the library.

There was one place where I could find out
who I was and what I was going to become.
And that was the Public Library.
JERZY KOSINSKI

Cambridge Public Library, Central Square Branch

CAMBRIDGE, MASSACHUSETTS

The kids had entered into the world of the story. Neither the librarian turning pages nor the presence of a photographer could bring them out of it.

. . . their grave eyes reflected the eternal fascination of the fairy tale: would the monster be bested . . . or would he feed?
STEPHEN KING

121

Newton Free Library

NEWTON, MASSACHUSETTS

The old library has since been torn down and an impressive, brightly lit modern one has replaced it, quite an achievement in this era of tax-cutting. But alas there are now no interesting dark corners, nor mysterious encounters in the stacks.

There were many hours when I never quite knew how I'd gotten there or why I stayed. —PHILIP ROTH

Billings Square Library

WORCESTER, MASSACHUSETTS

The building had been locked up for a while, one of six branches closed in 1990 for lack of funding, reflecting the budget cuts that are endangering many libraries. There have been more library closures (including school libraries) in the last couple of years than there were during the depression. It was a freezing fall day, there was no heat, and strong winds came in through the broken windows. Most of the books had been transferred to other libraries, and it was a forlorn scene.

Some kids go to the library . . . Others to the street. But they
can't go to the libraries if the libraries are closed.

OFFICER DOMBRANSKI, NYPD

Bibliothèque Nationale

PARIS, FRANCE

The glorious reading room took my breath away. It was built in 1862 by Henri Labrouste, who also built the Bibliothèque Sainte-Geneviève, and has nine domes, each with an "eye" providing natural light from above. The roof is supported with twelve slender iron columns. Currently an enormous modern library is nearing completion in Paris, the infamous TGB ("Très Grand Bibliothèque"), and the Bibliothèque Nationale is preparing to merge with it to become the Bibliothèque de France. Perhaps it will be a "very grand bibliothèque," but nothing can have the majesty or the grace of this one.

I have always imagined that Paradise will be a kind of library. —JORGE LUIS BORGES

Widener Library, Harvard University

CAMBRIDGE, MASSACHUSETTS

The stacks seem like such a natural place to bring heart and mind together. A former graduate has fond memories of them: "She (wife-to-be) was a senior, and we had access to the stacks. Study breaks and cuddling breaks (French History section), then alternated. To this day I have marks on my knees from crawling on the marble floors." (Perry Viles, Harvard 1954, Ph.D. 1965, Executive Director, St. Johnsbury Athenaeum, Vermont)

They kiss in cubicles; for all we know they
breed down there in the twelfth century.

LARRY RUBIN

LIBRARIES PHOTOGRAPHED

AUTHORS QUOTED

Angle, Paul McClelland, *The Library of Congress*
Bellow, Saul (found in *The Readers Quotation Book*)
Borges, Jorge Luis, "Poema de los Dones," *El Hacedor*
Bourbeau, Sheila, from *Historical Society of Cotuit*
Brennan, Michael, *The Boston Globe*, December 30, 1991
Brown, Rita Mae (found in *The Readers Quotation Book*)
Broyard, Anatole, *The New York Times Book Review*,
    February 22, 1987
Carlyle, Thomas
Cecil, Lord David, in *The London Library Book*
Cole William, *The Heart of the Heart of the Library*
Dana, John Cotton, in *Libraries: Addresses and Essays*
Dewey, Melvil, *Libraries in America*
Dombranski, Officer

Eliot, Charles W.
Emerson, Ralph Waldo
Fritz, Jean (found in *The Readers Quotation Book*)
Galbraith, John Kenneth
Giovanni, Nikki, "The Library," from *Brothers and
    Sisters*
Goodrum, Charles A., *Dewey Decimated*
Greer, Germaine, *Daddy, We Hardly Knew You*
Hamill, Pete, *D'Artaganan on Ninth Street*
Harley, Bill, *Memories of Mrs. Bergeson*
Hugo, Victor
Huxtable, Ada Louise
James I of England
Jarrell, Randall, *Children Selecting Books from a Library*

Johnson, Samuel

Joyce, James, *Ulysses*

Kaufman, Bel, *The Liberry*

Kazin, Alfred, *New York Jew*

King, Stephen, *It*

Kozinski, Jerzy, from *Testimonials* for the
New York Public Library

Laski, Harold J., *Holmes-Laski Letters*

Longfellow, Henry Wadsworth

MacLeish, Archibald, "The Premise of Meaning,"
American Scholar, June 5, 1972

Maddocks, Melvin, "Bookish," *World Monitor*,
August 1989

Malcolm X, *The Autobiography of Malcolm X*

Mallarmé, Stephane

McCullough, David, *Truman*

Morley, Christopher, *Pipefuls*

Rilke, Rainer Maria, (found in *The Readers
Quotation Book*)

Roth, Philip, *Goodbye Columbus*

Rubin, Larry, *The World's Old Way*

Russell, John, *New York Times*, November 30, 1986

Schopenhauer, Arthur, in *Books of the Western World*

Sévigné, Marie de,

Shakespeare, William, *Titus Andronicus*

Shuman, Bruce A., *Riverbend Revisited*

Singer, Isaac Bashevis

Smith, Alexander,

Toth, Susan Allen, *Reading Rooms*

Tuchman, Barbara, *New Yorker*, April 21, 1986

Waters, Michael, *Covert Street*

Weeks, Linton, *Washington Post Magazine*

Weltner, Linda, *No Place Like Home*

Wendorf, Richard

Whittier, John Greenleaf, *The Library*

Yourcenar, Marguerite, *Memoirs of Hadrian*